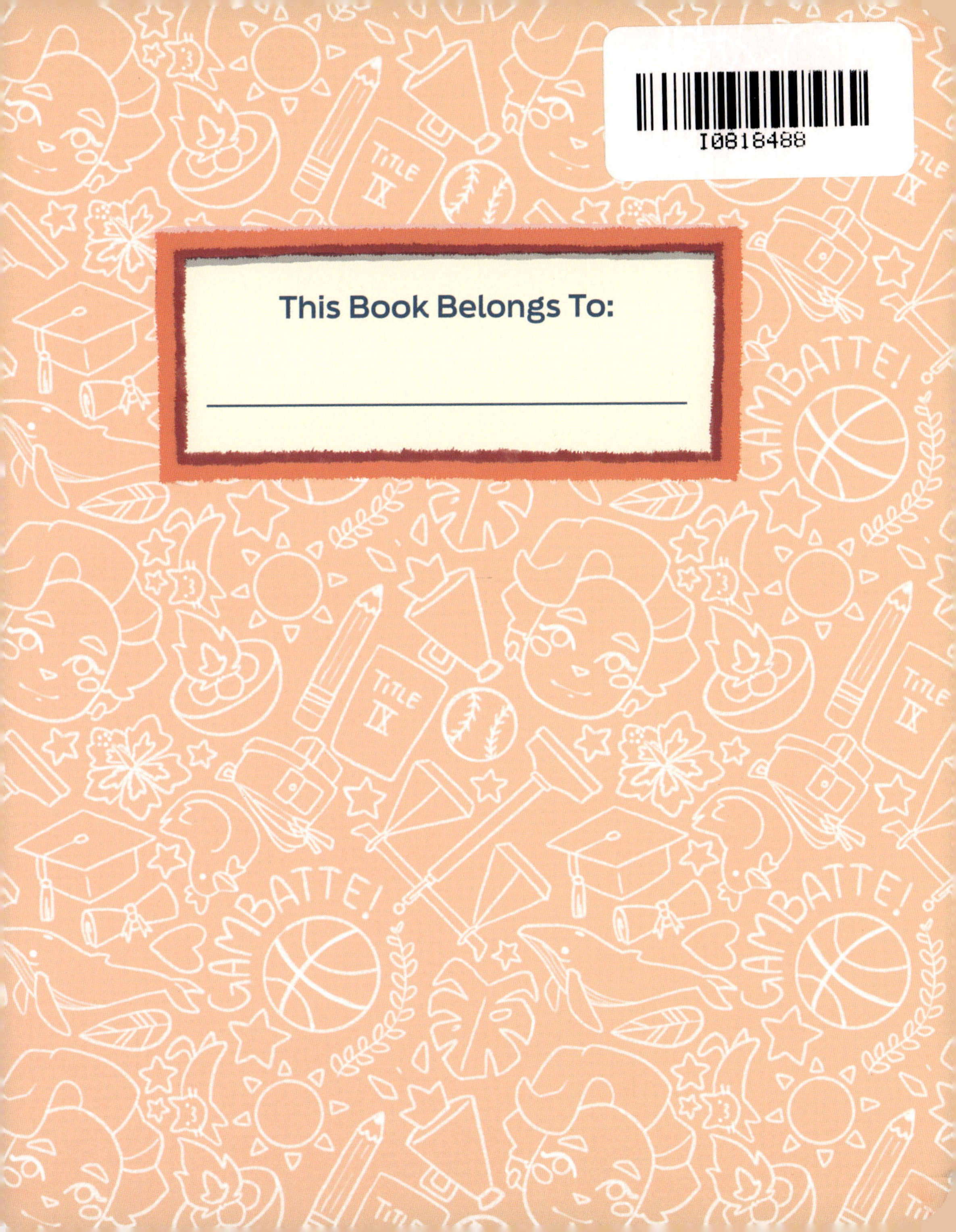

This Book Belongs To:
TITLE IX
GAMBATTE!

Wayfinders LITTLE BIOGRAPHIES OF HAWAI'I'S LEADERS

PATSY MINK

HAWAI'I'S CHAMPION FOR WOMEN'S RIGHTS

written by David Del Rocco

illustrated by Storm Kano

BeachHouse

Patsy Takemoto Mink was born on December 6, 1927, in a town called Pāʻia on the island of Maui.

Growing up on Maui, Patsy wanted to be a doctor. Back then, that was not what girls were expected to do, and people laughed at her for thinking she could be a doctor.

Patsy was best friends with her brother, Eugene, who was one year older than her. Their yard had a vegetable garden, a watermelon patch, mango and papaya trees, and a lily garden.

They also had cats, chickens, rabbits, and a dog. Patsy was a Girl Scout, and she also took piano lessons and hula lessons.

As a student at Maui High School, she won her first election and became class president. In 1944, she graduated as the valedictorian, which meant she was first in her class!

Patsy went to the University of Nebraska after high school. Because she was Japanese and not white, she was not allowed to live in the regular dorms. She began an antiracism campaign to protest this unfair treatment.

Patsy returned home to Hawaiʻi to finish her education at the University of Hawaiʻi and became the president of the Pre-Medicine Students Club.

After graduating from college, Patsy applied to several medical schools. She was not accepted to any of them. Some of them even told her that she was not accepted because she was a woman!

Instead of medicine, she decided to apply to law school and was accepted by the University of Chicago Law School. There, she met John Mink, the man who would become her husband. They got married in January of 1951 and had their daughter, Wendy, in 1952.

After she graduated with a law degree, no law firm would hire Patsy, but that didn't stop her. She started her own law practice and became the first Japanese American woman to practice law in Hawai'i. She also decided to run for office.

Patsy ran for the Territorial House of Representatives, and she won! As a territorial representative, Patsy pushed for something that many people in Hawaiʻi wanted: statehood.

On August 11, 1958, Patsy, along with her husband and daughter, drove out into the night to witness an atomic bombing test. The US Navy was dropping bombs on a Pacific island called Johnston Atoll.

As the family watched from the island of O'ahu, they could see the bright flash and colorful cloud from the explosion, even though Johnston Atoll was over 800 miles away.

September 1964

DAILY NEWS

“GAMBATTE!”

Patsy T. Mink Elected!!!

Gambatte is a Japanese word that means “go for it” and “do your best.” This was Patsy’s favorite cheer whenever she was going to tackle something big and important, such as running for Congress or fighting racism.

After Hawai‘i became the fiftieth state in 1959, Patsy ran for Congress but lost to Senator Daniel Inouye. She didn't give up. She ran again in 1964 and won! Patsy and her family made the big move to Washington, DC.

Patsy was the youngest member from the youngest state and the first Japanese American woman elected to Congress. She worked hard on issues that helped children and promoted education. And she fought for equal rights for women.

In 1969, a 500-pound unexploded bomb was found on Maui, Patsy Mink's home island. Now a US representative, Patsy called for the Navy to stop the bombing of Kaho'olawe. Sadly, the bombing of the island did not end until 1990.

Years later, Patsy worked on environmental issues under President Carter to protect our oceans from deep-sea mining and toxic waste, and to protect our whales.

Patsy was no stranger to discrimination. She faced it many times in her life because she was a woman and because she was Asian. She fought against injustice whenever she saw it. What she is the most famous for is Title IX (pronounced nine). This law prohibits discrimination based on someone's gender.

This opened up a whole new world of sports and education for girls and women. Many male athletes were worried that men's sports would receive less money and attention if there were sports just for women, but Congress voted, and in 1972, Title IX became a reality.

TITLE IX
$a^2 + b^2 = c^2$
a
a = 5
b = 7
c
b

Although Patsy left this world in 2002, she left a wonderful legacy that still benefits thousands of women and girls. Title IX was renamed in her honor as the Patsy Mink Equal Opportunity in Education Act.

US Representative and House Minority Leader Richard Gephardt said, "This strong-willed woman changed the face of America forever."

We will always remember this
remarkable woman.

Glossary

Territorial—belonging to the territory of Hawai'i. (Before Hawai'i became the fiftieth state, it was called a "territory" meaning it was not a state, but it belonged to the US.)

Discrimination—being treated unfairly; for example, not being chosen for a job or not being allowed to do something because of your race or gender.

Injustice—unfair treatment.

Prohibits—does not allow something to happen.

Sources

Alexander, Kerri Lee. National Women's History Museum, Charlotte, NC
https://www.womenshistory.org/education-resources/biographies/patsy-mink

Kua, Crystal. *Honolulu Star-Bulletin,* Oct. 4, 2002
https://archives.starbulletin.com/2002/10/04/news/story2.html

Mink, Gwendolyn. E-mail exchange, December, 2023

Mink! (film) Breakwater Studios, Los Angeles, CA, 2022

Patsy Mink: Ahead of the Majority (film), Making Waves Films, Honolulu, HI, 2008

Protect Kaho'olawe 'Ohana, Kaunakakai, HI
http://www.protectkahoolaweohana.org/

Wu, Judy Tzu-Chun and Gwendolyn Mink. *Fierce and Fearless.* New York University Press: New York, NY, 2022

About the Author

David Del Rocco is a high school teacher who lives and works in Honolulu. He has a BA in the Hawaiian Language from the University of Hawaiʻi, a BA in Spanish from Rutgers University, and an MLIS from the University of Hawaiʻi.

About the Illustrator

Storm Kano is a published illustrator of local children's books. Born and raised on Oʻahu, she hopes to give back to her community through the art of visual storytelling. When she's not drawing, Storm enjoys exploring the natural beauty of the island and cuddling with her dog, Toby. For more information, visit www.StormKano.art.

ISBN: 978-1-949000-35-1
Library of Congress Control Number: 2024935204

Illustrations by Storm Kano
Design by Jane Gillespie
First Printing, August 2024

BeachHouse Publishing
PO Box 5464 • Kāneʻohe, Hawaiʻi 96744
info@beachhousepublishing.com
www.beachhousepublishing.com

Printed in China

Follow us on Instagram!

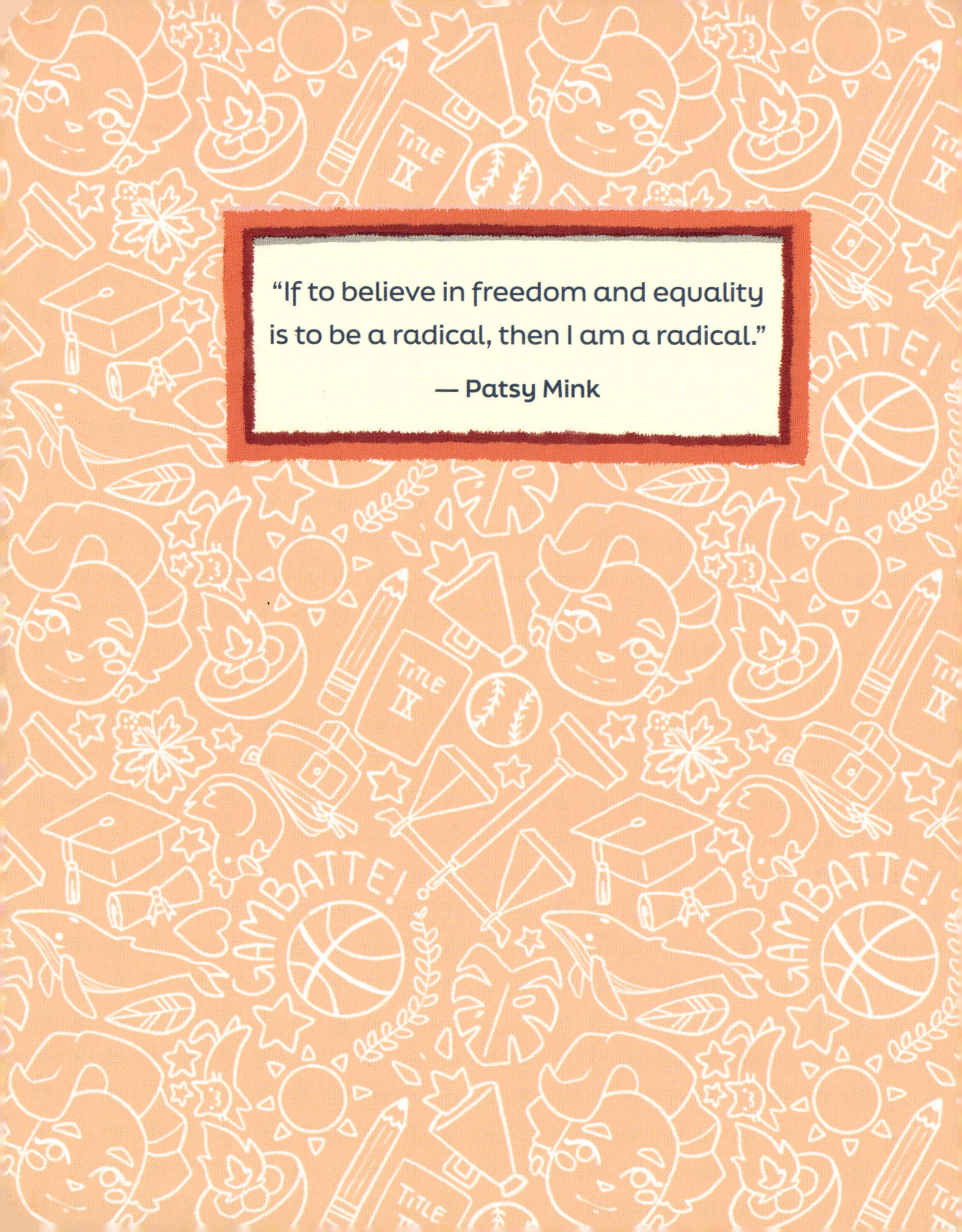
"If to believe in freedom and equality is to be a radical, then I am a radical."
— Patsy Mink